THE MATANUSKA COLONY ALBUM

PHOTOGRAPHS OF THE 1935 MATANUSKA
COLONY PROJECT IN PALMER, ALASKA

Helen Hegener

NORTHERN LIGHT MEDIA

THE MATANUSKA COLONY ALBUM

The Matanuska Colony Album

Photographs of the 1935 Matanuska Colony Project

by Helen Hegener

© 2014 Helen Hegener, Northern Light Media. All Rights Reserved. No part of this book may be reproduced or transmitted in any form or by any means, electronic or mechanical, including photocopying, recording, or by any information storage and retrieval system, in whole or in part, without written permission from the the author and publisher, except for brief passages for the purpose of reviewing this book.

First printing 2014 by Northern Light Media.
Printed in the United States of America.

ISBN-13 978-0-9843977-9-2
ISBN-10 0-9843977-9-5

For additional copies of this book
send $20.00 plus $4.00 postage to:

Northern Light Media
PO Box 298023
Wasilla, Alaska 99629

http://northernlightmedia.wordpress.com

THE MATANUSKA COLONY ALBUM

"I never dreamed it was as nice as what we saw when we got here."
~ Ray Rebarchek, Colonist

Photo above: Julia Dingman, young colonist daughter, keeps almost as many raspberries in her mouth as she does in her pail. [Willis T. Geisman ASL-P270-716 Mary Nan Gamble Collection, Alaska State Library]

Photo page 5: Mail Day in front of Palmer Post Office and Felton's General Store. [Willis T. Geisman ASL-P270-553 Mary Nan Gamble Collection, Alaska State Library]

THE MATANUSKA COLONY ALBUM

A group of the colonists' children that play in the streets at Camp 8.
[Willis T. Geisman ASL-P270-609 Mary Nan Gamble Collection, Alaska State Library]

"Creaking winches and groaning cargo booms hummed the overture here yesterday to another American epic of adventure and pioneering - the impending departure of a new band of pilgrims for a promised land."

-The Christian Science Monitor
San Francisco, California, April 22, 1935

THE MATANUSKA COLONY ALBUM

The Matanuska Colony Album

Photographs of the 1935 Matanuska Colony Project, Palmer, Alaska

6 ~ Introduction • Willis T. Geisman

10 ~ The Matanuska Colony Project

16 ~ Voyage of the North Star

30 ~ Laying the Groundwork

42 ~ First Colonists Arrive

50 ~ Second Contingent

82 ~ Colony Life

122 ~ The Transient Workmen

128 ~ Colony Legacies

146 ~ Bibliography

THE MATANUSKA COLONY ALBUM

Willis T. Geisman 1935

Introduction

On April 23, 1935, the Bureau of Indian Affairs ship North Star, chartered from the Department of the Interior by the Federal Emergency Relief Administration, left San Francisco bound for Seward, Alaska. On board was a large contingent of administrators, staff, and construction supervisors charged with laying the groundwork for the Matanuska Colony Project.

General Manager Don Irwin, Director of Construction Col. Frank Bliss, his staff, and many others, including an architect, an engineer, a physician and many more who would play key roles in the government's bold New Deal experiment in Alaska, were transporting the tents, stoves, trucks, tractors, well-drilling equipment and other materials necessary for creating a new community in the Alaskan wilderness. Also on board were 118 transient workmen, the first group of several hundred who would be building the homes, barns, administrative buildings and roads for the new colony.

Joining this advance guard as the official photographer was an earnest young graduate from the University of California at Berkeley named Willis Taubert Geisman, who played rugby and had lettered in Political Science. Even before setting sail, Geisman photographed the Emergency Relief Administration headquarters on 4th Street in San Francisco, tractors and equipment arriving by train, and the loading of trucks and farm machinery onto the North Star at Pier 50.

As the official photographer for the Matanuska Colony Project, Geisman documented every aspect of the venture, from the kitchen help aboard the North Star to the colonists' children playing in the tent city, from officials posing stiffly for portraits to transient workmen and farmers working together to build their homes before winter. His photographs portray a proud farm wife showing off her neat tent kitchen, and a small girl sitting in an Alaskan berry patch grinning at the cameraman.

On the cover of his Official Photographic Album of the Alaska Rural Rehabilitation Corporation, Matanuska Colonization Project, which contains 939 black and white photographs, Geisman noted: "Complete Album photographed and produced in the field with portable equipment by Willis T. Geisman, official photographer, ARRC Palmer, Alaska, 1935."

Little is known about Willis Geisman's life. He was born in San Francisco on November 1, 1911, to Clarence John and Florence N. Geisman. At some point in his life he married, and he joined the Marine Corps, where he attained the rank of Captain in the 4th Marine Regiment.

Only seven years after sailing to Alaska on the North Star, on May 6, 1942, Willis Geisman was captured by the Japanese after the fall of Corregidor in the Philippine Islands, and he was held as a prisoner of war until his death while still in captivity. Burial was at the Manila American Cemetery and Memorial, Manila, Philippines. His posthumous awards included the Prisoner of War Medal and the Purple Heart.

Willis Geisman's thorough documentation of the 1935 Matanuska Colony project was a monumental achievement, and has become the single most frequently referenced work on that uniquely important part of Alaska's history. His compelling photographs of the Colony have appeared in hundreds of books, magazines, news articles, on television, and in films.

Willis Geisman's outstanding photographs played a major role in the award-winning 2008 documentary film about the Matanuska Colony Project, *Alaska Far Away*. Valley historian Jim Fox, author of the out-of-print book, *The First Summer*, a splendid collection of some of Geisman's most memorable photographs presented in a large format, wrote: "Geisman's work is of tremendous importance in its documentation of the Colony's history and its technical skill, artistic, and documentary style."

Willis Geisman's work during the first six months of the Matanuska Colony left an incredible photographic legacy for Alaskans. He not only captured the Matanuska Colony Project in all of its variables, but he also recorded the important work being done at the Matanuska Experiment Station in agricultural advancements, and he captured some of the only photographs of many of the early pioneer farmers of the Matanuska Valley.

Willis Geisman photographed early-day Anchorage from the air, and recorded the flooding of the town of Matanuska, which no longer exists. He photographed smiles, frowns, wonderment, puzzlement, sadness, joy and a hundred other moods on the faces of Alaskans going about their daily lives almost eight decades ago.

With his 939 photographs, only a handful of which are reproduced in this book, Willis T. Geisman left an invaluable historic treasure for all Alaskans.

THE MATANUSKA COLONY ALBUM

Pioneer Peak, six thousand foot sentinel that watches over Matanuska Valley.
[Willis T. Geisman ASL-P270-667 Mary Nan Gamble Collection, Alaska State Library]

THE MATANUSKA COLONY ALBUM

In Alaska the pots of gold are many, for during the
rainy season rainbows are every day occurrences.
[Willis T. Geisman ASL-P270-667 Mary Nan Gamble Collection, Alaska State Library]

"Geisman's work is of tremendous importance in its documentation of the Colony's history and its technical skill, artistic and documentary style." ~Jim Fox, author of The Last Summer

The Matanuska Colony Project

Alaska's dramatically beautiful Matanuska Valley sits at the head of Knik Arm, crossed by three major rivers and surrounded by towering mountains on three sides. Today it is the state's agricultural heartland, and that is the ongoing legacy of the 1935 Matanuska Colony Project.

The picturesque farms with their soaring-roofed Colony barns are historic landmarks, and reminders of an all-but-forgotten chapter in American history, when the U.S. government rolled the dice and offered 203 Depression-distraught families an opportunity to begin their lives over again, with government financing and support, in this wild land.

The Matanuska Colony Project was part of President Franklin Delano Roosevelt's optimistically grandiose New Deal, a series of economic programs designed to provide the "3 R's": Relief, Recovery, and Reform."

THE MATANUSKA COLONY ALBUM

Relief for the poor and the unemployed, Recovery of the economy to normal levels, and Reform of the financial system to prevent a repeat depression. It was an era of outlandish programs dreamed up by bold visionaries, but none were bolder or more outlandish than the Matanuska Colony Project.

The Matanuska Colony was not the only government rural rehabilitation project; it was in fact only one of a multitude of complex, ambitious and controversial programs initiated under Franklin Roosevelt's New Deal Federal Rural Development Program. Other resettlement projects included Dyess Colony, Arkansas; Arthurdale, West Virginia; the Phoenix Homesteads in Arizona; and similar colonies in over a dozen other states.

In his 1968 book, *The Colorful Matanuska Valley*, author and General Manager of the Matanuska Colony Project, Don L. Irwin, explained, "On February 4, 1935, President Roosevelt, by Executive Order No. 6957, withdrew an area of 8,000 acres in the Matanuska Valley from homestead entry. This area was supplemented by a March 13 withdrawal of 18,000 acres of grazing land. Both of these withdrawals were for the benefit of the Colony Project."

The areas withdrawn lie generally along both sides of the lower reaches of the Matanuska River in the eastern part of the Valley. Irwin detailed the early days of the Matanuska Valley, noting, "There were approximately 100 miles of graded road in the Valley in the spring of 1935. Not more than 20 miles was gravel surfaced and none of it was paved. There was no road from the Valley into Anchorage."

Irwin went on to explain there was weekly freight and passenger service on the Alaska Railroad, but no more than 1,200 acres of land cleared of timber and under cultivation. "One married couple and three elderly bachelors comprised the population of

THE MATANUSKA COLONY ALBUM

Echo Lake on windless day.
[Willis T. Geisman ASL-P270-665 Mary Nan
Gamble Collection, Alaska State Library]

THE MATANUSKA COLONY ALBUM

Sjodin Colony barn on Scott Road, north of Palmer.
[Artwork by Susan L. Patch, from a photo by Helen Hegener]

Palmer. There was no doctor, nor were there hospital facilities in the Valley."

It was into this frontier setting the U.S. government brought their recruited settlers. With thousands answering the call, 203 families were eventually selected and transported to Alaska from the upper midwestern states of Michigan, Minnesota, and Wisconsin, as the project planners guessed that residents of these northern tier states would be most familiar with the harsh climate conditions which would be found in Alaska. The colonists arrived in two contingents, the first, being the families from Minnesota, arrived on May 10; the second contingent, families from Michigan and Wisconsin, arrived two weeks later, on May 24.

Although fraught with inevitable bureaucratic entanglements, frustrating delays, personality clashes and a myriad of other distractions, the Matanuska Colony actually thrived for the most part, and the majority of the families remained to raise their families and make their permanent homes in Alaska. Highways were built, the wide Matanuska and Knik Rivers were bridged, and the town of Palmer became the center of commerce and society in the Valley. By 1948, production from the Colony Project farms provided over half of the total Alaskan agricultural products sold.

Today the Matanuska Valley draws worldwide attention for its colorful agricultural heritage and its uniquely orchestrated history. The iconic Colony barn, often seen around the Valley now in artwork, logos, advertising and other uses, has become a beloved symbol of this unique chapter in Alaska's history.

Author's notes appear in italics in the photo captions.

THE MATANUSKA COLONY ALBUM

The Voyage of the North Star - U.S.M.S. North Star in dock at Pier 50, Port of San Francisco, April 20, 1935. [Willis T. Geisman ASL-P270-001 Mary Nan Gamble Collection, Alaska State Library] *The North Star left San Francisco on April 23, 1935, transporting the administrative staff, construction workers, and materials for the colony.*

One of the fifteen Ford trucks taken to Alaska. Truck suspended by cables over ship. Several men in background. [Willis T. Geisman ASL-P270-008 Mary Nan Gamble Collection, Alaska State Library]

THE MATANUSKA COLONY ALBUM

First Contingent Staff. (Top row, L to R) Earl Stacy, Cook; Jean White, Cook; Ben Jordan, Steward; Eugene Sedille, General Foreman; Charles Richards, Quartermaster; Clyde Peck, Machinist; Hovey Stoneman, Asst. Quartermaster; Willis Geisman, Photographer; Albert Snell, Superintendent; Dr. Earl Ostrom, Physician; Frank V. Bliss, Director; Frank. G. Carr, Secretary; Earl Osburn, Nurse; George Reuter, Accountant [posing aboard ship]. [Willis T. Geisman ASL-P270-015 Mary Nan Gamble Collection, Alaska State Library]

THE MATANUSKA COLONY ALBUM

Colonist Division Officials. (L to R) Steward Campbell, Property Custodian; Frank V. Bliss, Director of Construction; Don L. Irwin, General Manager, A.R.R.C.; Francis L. Biggs, Engineer [seated aboard ship]. [Willis T. Geisman ASL-P270-016 Mary Nan Gamble Collection, Alaska State Library]

THE MATANUSKA COLONY ALBUM

Enrollees aboard ship. Group of men on deck. [Willis T. Geisman
ASL-P270-024 Mary Nan Gamble Collection, Alaska State Library]
The enrollees, or transient workmen, were recruited from the Federal transient camps in California; only unmarried men were accepted.

THE MATANUSKA COLONY ALBUM

Enrollees aboard ship. Three men playing cards on deck. [Willis T. Geisman
ASL-P270-022 Mary Nan Gamble Collection, Alaska State Library]
*To ensure the transient workmen would leave Alaska after the work was completed, they
would not be paid more than $2.00 per week until they had returned as far as Seattle.*

Loading the NORTH STAR at Ketchikan. View of lumber stacked alongside ship. Building sign in background: Heckman Wharf. [Willis T. Geisman ASL-P270-043 Mary Nan Gamble Collection, Alaska State Library]

THE MATANUSKA COLONY ALBUM

Roll call previous to departure from Ketchikan, May 2nd [1935]. [Willis T. Geisman ASL-P270-044 Mary Nan Gamble Collection, Alaska State Library]

Loading crate onto North Star in Juneau. [Willis T. Geisman ASL-P270-055 Mary Nan Gamble Collection, Alaska State Library]

Men stacking and securing lumber on deck of North Star. [Willis T. Geisman ASL-P270-062 Mary Nan Gamble Collection, Alaska State Library]

THE MATANUSKA COLONY ALBUM

Enrollees leaving the NORTH STAR, 6 a.m., May 6th [1935] in a pouring rain. Man carrying gear. [Willis T. Geisman ASL-P270-066 Mary Nan Gamble Collection, Alaska State Library]

Enrollees aboard train at Seward. Interior of passenger car. [Willis T. Geisman ASL-P270-071 Mary Nan Gamble Collection, Alaska State Library]

Train holding first contingent transients climbing the mountains after leaving Seward, May 6th [1935]. View of front of train rounding a snowy curve. [Willis T. Geisman ASL-P270-072 Mary Nan Gamble Collection, Alaska State Library]

Changing trains at Anchorage. Men gathering baggage beside train. [Willis T. Geisman ASL-P270-077 Mary Nan Gamble Collection, Alaska State Library]

First contingent staff as they arrived at Matanuska, 4:30 p.m., May 6th [1935]. Eleven men posing in front of train station. [Willis T. Geisman ASL-P270-078 Mary Nan Gamble Collection, Alaska State Library] *The town of Matanuska, which no longer exists, had a population of around 50 people, with a general store, a liquor store, a roadhouse, a post office, a grade school and a high school, a dance and meeting hall, and the Alaska Railroad station, as seen in the photo.*

THE MATANUSKA COLONY ALBUM

(L to R) Snell, Campbell, [unidentified], Biggs, Sheely, Bliss. Standing on dirt road; forest in background. [Willis T. Geisman ASL-P270-079 Mary Nan Gamble Collection, Alaska State Library]

The welcoming committee walking down the road at Palmer. May 6th [1935]. [Willis T. Geisman ASL-P270-080 Mary Nan Gamble Collection, Alaska State Library]

THE MATANUSKA COLONY ALBUM

(L to R) Sheely, Biggs and Bliss survey blue prints upon arrival at Palmer. [Willis T. Geisman ASL-P270-081 Mary Nan Gamble Collection, Alaska State Library]
Ross Sheely, administrative assistant; Francis Biggs, Engineer; Frank V. Bliss, Director of Construction for the Matanuska Colony Project.

THE MATANUSKA COLONY ALBUM

Site of colonists' camp No. 1 before construction May 7th [1935]. Pickup truck in foreground. [Willis T. Geisman ASL-P270-084 Mary Nan Gamble Collection, Alaska State Library]

THE MATANUSKA COLONY ALBUM

Floors and first tent frames erected for colonists' tents, 11:30 p.m., May 7th [1935]. [Willis T. Geisman ASL-P270-088 Mary Nan Gamble Collection, Alaska State Library]

Tent construction, Palmer. View of frames and completed tents. [Willis T. Geisman ASL-P270-089 Mary Nan Gamble Collection, Alaska State Library]

Base Hospital. Row of 4 tents with American Flag and Red Cross flag. [Willis T. Geisman ASL-P270-101 Mary Nan Gamble Collection, Alaska State Library]

Tank at Camp No. 1. Well rig and water tank. [Willis T. Geisman ASL-P270-110 Mary Nan Gamble Collection, Alaska State Library]

THE MATANUSKA COLONY ALBUM

Camp from top of water tank.

Camp from top of water tank. 2 rows of tents. [Willis T. Geisman ASL-P270-112 Mary Nan Gamble Collection, Alaska State Library]

Temporary kitchen for Construction Division. Two stoves set up by the railroad tracks. [Willis T. Geisman ASL-P270-116 Mary Nan Gamble Collection, Alaska State Library]

THE MATANUSKA COLONY ALBUM

Temporary mess. Close-up of a man being served from small stove. [Willis T. Geisman ASL-P270-117 Mary Nan Gamble Collection, Alaska State Library]

THE COLONISTS' ARRIVAL AT PALMER 5:20 PM, May 10th, 1935. Mrs. Elvi Kerttula with daughter Esther disembarking from train on arrival. [Willis T. Geisman ASL-P270-124 Mary Nan Gamble Collection, Alaska State Library]

Colonists going to their tents. [Willis T. Geisman ASL-P270-130 Mary Nan Gamble Collection, Alaska State Library]

Corduroy road construction across ravine at Camp 8. [Willis T. Geisman ASL-P270-145 Mary Nan Gamble Collection, Alaska State Library]
Corduroy roads were a common way of dealing with wet or swampy conditions in roadbuilding in early Alaska.

THE MATANUSKA COLONY ALBUM

Camp 8 showing corduroy road, tents and well rig. May 29th [1935]. [Willis T. Geisman ASL-P270-146 Mary Nan Gamble Collection, Alaska State Library]
Camp #8 was about two miles south of Palmer, near the Matanuska River.

Well diggers at work. May 10th [1935]. Two men cranking a windlass over a hole in the ground. [Willis T. Geisman ASL-P270-165 Mary Nan Gamble Collection, Alaska State Library]

Knut Johnson, local well digger. Looking down on Johnson in the bottom of a wood-lined shaft. [Willis T. Geisman ASL-P270-166 Mary Nan Gamble Collection, Alaska State Library]

THE MATANUSKA COLONY ALBUM

First church services held in the colony. 11 a.m. May 12, 1935. Mother's Day. Rev. B. J. Bingle. [Willis T. Geisman ASL-P270-179 Mary Nan Gamble Collection, Alaska State Library]

THE MATANUSKA COLONY ALBUM

Raising old Glory for the first time over the Hospital. May 19, 1935 (L to R) W. Hawkins, nurse; Dr. E. A. Ostrom; Earl Ostrom [Osburn], nurse; Red Cross nurse, Madeleine de Foras. [Willis T. Geisman ASL-P270-181 Mary Nan Gamble Collection, Alaska State Library]

THE MATANUSKA COLONY ALBUM

ST. MIHIEL drops anchor at Seward, 8 a.m., May 22nd, 1935. [Willis T. Geisman ASL-P270-186 Mary Nan Gamble Collection, Alaska State Library]
The families from Michigan and Wisconsin were aboard the St. Mihiel.

THE MATANUSKA COLONY ALBUM

An Alaskan husky greets the newcomers at Seward. Children on board reaching out to dog on dock. [Willis T. Geisman ASL-P270-194 Mary Nan Gamble Collection, Alaska State Library]

ST. MIHIEL officers assist the colonists. [Willis T. Geisman ASL-P270-198 Mary Nan Gamble Collection, Alaska State Library]

THE MATANUSKA COLONY ALBUM

School buses being unloaded. Bus suspended from crane. [Willis T. Geisman ASL-P270-204 Mary Nan Gamble Collection, Alaska State Library]

Mothers and babies arriving at Matanuska [train station]. Margaret Nelson with daughter Norma and a camera. [Willis T. Geisman ASL-P270-225 Mary Nan Gamble Collection, Alaska State Library]

THE MATANUSKA COLONY ALBUM

Matanuska colonists at railroad station, Palmer. [Willis T. Geisman ASL-P270-224 Mary Nan Gamble Collection, Alaska State Library]

Don L. Irwin raps for order as the drawing starts. On platform above crowd. [Willis T. Geisman ASL-P270-211 Mary Nan Gamble Collection, Alaska State Library] *The colonists drew slips of paper to determine where the tracts of land for their farms would be located, most parcels were 40 acres, a few were 80 acres.*

THE MATANUSKA COLONY ALBUM

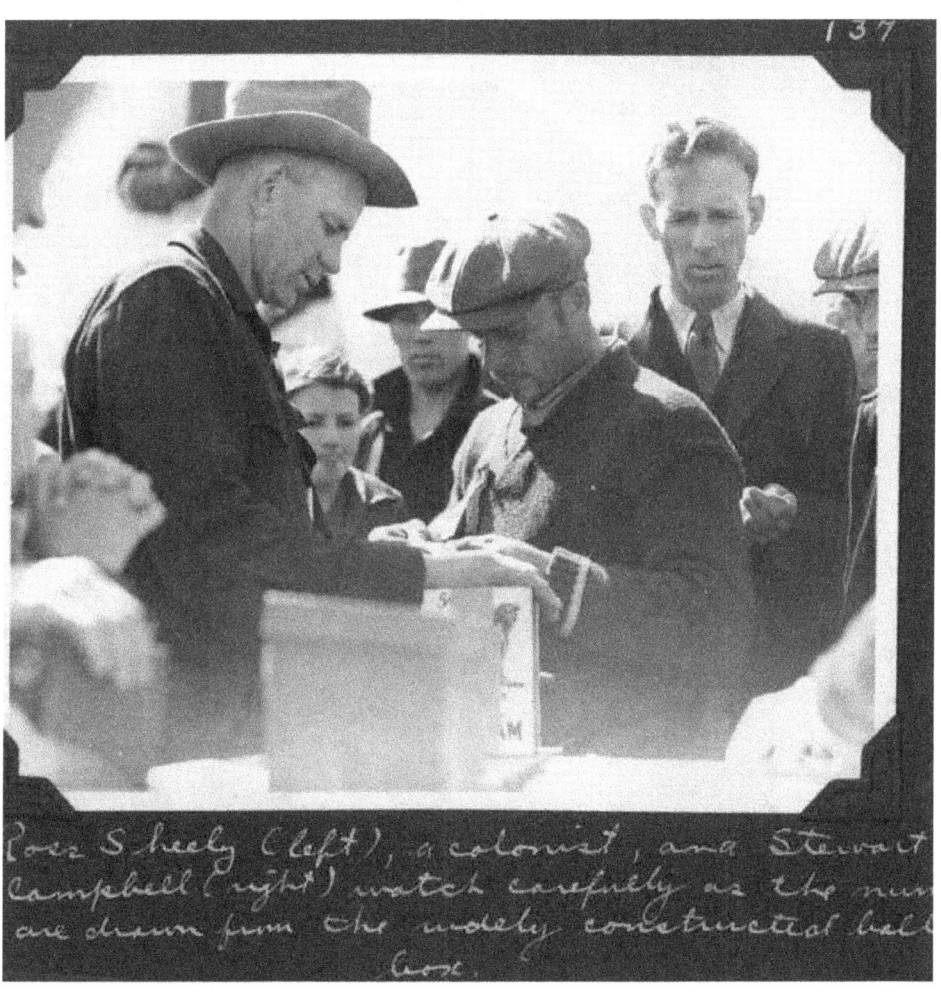

Ross Sheely (left), a colonist, and Stewart Campbell (right) watch carefully as the numbers are drawn from the rudely constructed ballot box. [Willis T. Geisman ASL-P270-218 Mary Nan Gamble Collection, Alaska State Library]
Ross Sheely and Stewart Campbell were both administrative assistants.

THE MATANUSKA COLONY ALBUM

Unloading Ford pickups at Palmer. [Willis T. Geisman ASL-P270-920 Mary Nan Gamble Collection, Alaska State Library]

Transient men leaving by truck for their day's work, 7:30 a.m. [Willis T. Geisman ASL-P270-884 Mary Nan Gamble Collection, Alaska State Library]

THE MATANUSKA COLONY ALBUM

June 8th [1935]. Cabin nearing completion and flying U.S. flag, with mountains in background. [Willis T. Geisman ASL-P270-242 Mary Nan Gamble Collection, Alaska State Library]
This building would be the construction headquarters.

THE MATANUSKA COLONY ALBUM

Joseph Puhl, assisted by three neighbors, progresses rapidly on his cabin. Collection notes: ?, Arvid Johnson or Henning Benson with pipe, Virgil Eckert with adz, Joe Puhl, right. [Willis T. Geisman ASL-P270-293 Mary Nan Gamble Collection, Alaska State Library]

THE MATANUSKA COLONY ALBUM

Saw mill at Camp 5. Mill and lumberyard. [Willis T. Geisman ASL-P270-313 Mary Nan Gamble Collection, Alaska State Library]
Camp #5 was located about four miles northwest of Palmer.

THE MATANUSKA COLONY ALBUM

Hauling logs to the mill. [Willis T. Geisman ASL-P270-932 Mary Nan Gamble Collection, Alaska State Library]

Colonist running saw mill. [Willis T. Geisman ASL-P270-918 Mary Nan Gamble Collection, Alaska State Library]

THE MATANUSKA COLONY ALBUM

Cabin No. 140. [Willis T. Geisman ASL-P270-322 Mary Nan Gamble Collection, Alaska State Library]
Cabin no. 140 was built for the Earl Barry family, about two miles northwest of Palmer.

Cabin No. 148. [Willis T. Geisman ASL-P270-350 Mary Nan Gamble Collection, Alaska State Library]
Cabin no. 148 was built about two miles northwest of Palmer.

Frame Cottage No. 93. [Willis T. Geisman ASL-P270-355 Mary Nan Gamble Collection, Alaska State Library]
Cottage no. 93 was built about a mile northwest of Palmer, on Scott Road.

Camp No. 10. Construction Camp at the Butte. [Willis T. Geisman ASL-P270-457 Mary Nan Gamble Collection, Alaska State Library]
Camp no. 10 was on the west side of the Bodenburg Butte.

Cabin construction with the numbered logs. Note 2x8's cut at the mill being used for floor construction. [Willis T. Geisman ASL-P270-479 Mary Nan Gamble Collection, Alaska State Library] *Bodenburg Butte in background.*

Workmen drilling holes for pins. Man astride cabin wall with drilling apparatus. [Willis T. Geisman ASL-P270-482 Mary Nan Gamble Collection, Alaska State Library]

Driving pins into logs. [Willis T. Geisman ASL-P270-483 Mary Nan Gamble Collection, Alaska State Library]

THE MATANUSKA COLONY ALBUM

Pulling up logs for gable construction. [Willis T. Geisman ASL-P270-484 Mary Nan Gamble Collection, Alaska State Library]

Completed cabin (No. 178). All of the logs cut and numbered at the mill; it takes four men two days (10 hrs. each) to put up the log walls, and four men oneand a half days to put the gables. [Willis T. Geisman ASL-P270-485 Mary Nan Gamble Collection, Alaska State Library] *Cabin no. 178 was built for the Paul Nelson family on the south side of Bodenburg Butte.*

Colonists hauling logs to their cabin sites. [Willis T. Geisman ASL-P270-486 Mary Nan Gamble Collection, Alaska State Library]

THE MATANUSKA COLONY ALBUM

Trading-post construction at the civic center. [Willis T. Geisman ASL-P270-490 Mary Nan Gamble Collection, Alaska State Library]

One of the three shovels of the Alaska Road Commission at work. [Willis T. Geisman ASL-P270-510 Mary Nan Gamble Collection, Alaska State Library]

THE MATANUSKA COLONY ALBUM

Hauling gravel for road construction. [Willis T. Geisman ASL-P270-924 Mary Nan Gamble Collection, Alaska State Library]

Modern pioneers going down the main street at Palmer. Caterpillar and trailer are the only practical form of transportation over some of the roads. [Willis T. Geisman ASL-P270-528 Mary Nan Gamble Collection, Alaska State Library]

"A Matanuska Taxi" traveling on the newly constructed Anchorage Matanuska Highway. [Willis T. Geisman ASL-P270-529 Mary Nan Gamble Collection, Alaska State Library] *Pioneer Peak in the background.*

THE MATANUSKA COLONY ALBUM

Tent offices and warehouses. [
Willis T. Geisman ASL-P270-574 Mary Nan Gamble Collection, Alaska State Library]

THE MATANUSKA COLONY ALBUM

Tents used by officials and employees of the colonists' division. [Willis T. Geisman ASL-P270-575 Mary Nan Gamble Collection, Alaska State Library]

THE MATANUSKA COLONY ALBUM

A daily street scene.
[Willis T. Geisman ASL-P270-590 Mary Nan Gamble Collection, Alaska State Library]
The building is the Palmer post office and Felton's General Store.

THE MATANUSKA COLONY ALBUM

The tent city at Palmer.
[Willis T. Geisman ASL-P270-591 Mary Nan Gamble Collection, Alaska State Library]
The building on right is the Palmer post office and Felton's General Store.

Buddy and Victor Yohn at play in their new cabin. [Willis T. Geisman ASL-P270-593 Mary Nan Gamble Collection, Alaska State Library]

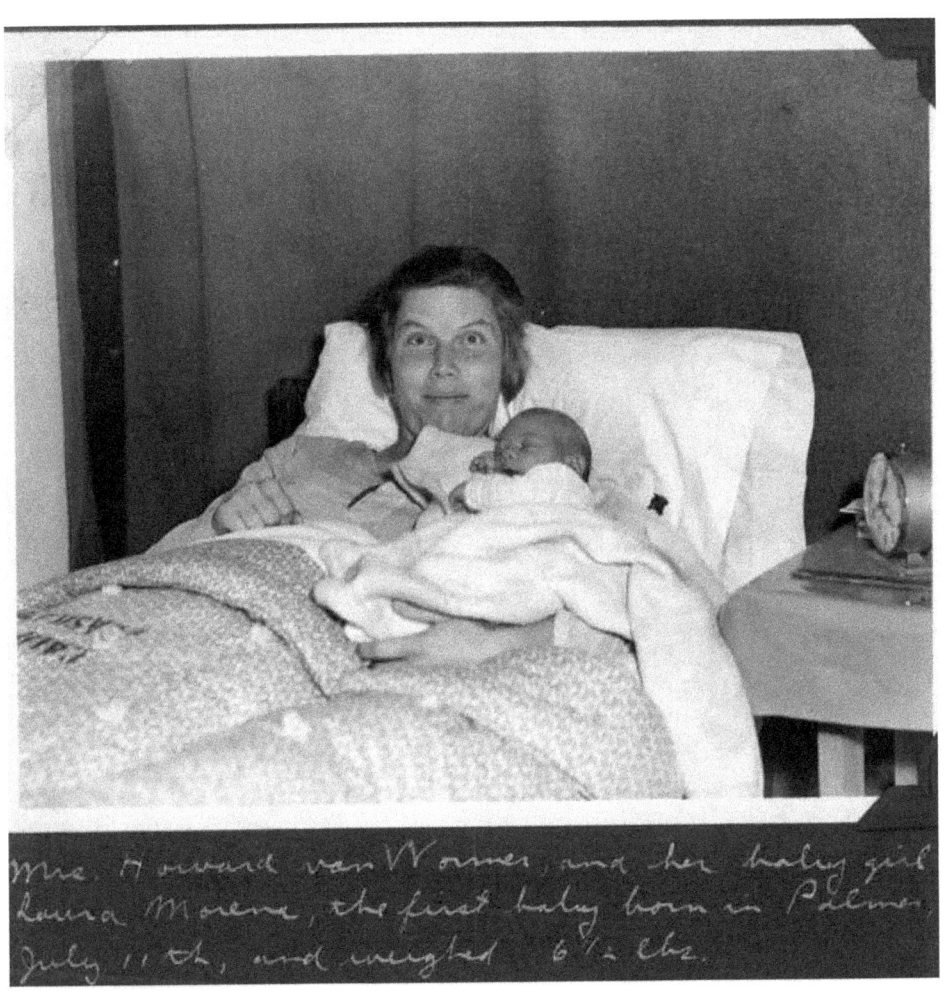

Mrs. Howard van Wormer and her baby girl, Laura Morena, the first baby born in Palmer, July 11th and weighed 6-1/2 lbs. [Willis T. Geisman ASL-P270-598 Mary Nan Gamble Collection, Alaska State Library]

Colonists' picnic and barbecue, 4th of July [1935]. [Willis T. Geisman ASL-P270-606 Mary Nan Gamble Collection, Alaska State Library]

THE MATANUSKA COLONY ALBUM

A group of the colonists' children that play in the streets at Camp 8. [Willis T. Geisman ASL-P270-609 Mary Nan Gamble Collection, Alaska State Library]

THE MATANUSKA COLONY ALBUM

The colonists' commissary. [Willis T. Geisman ASL-P270-610 Mary Nan Gamble Collection, Alaska State Library]

Publicized pioneers. Although it has been four months since the arrival of the colonists, newsmen and photographers are still prevalent. [Willis T. Geisman ASL-P270-613 Mary Nan Gamble Collection, Alaska State Library]

Arville Shaleben [Schaleben], reporter and photographer, MILWAUKEE JOURNAL. [Willis T. Geisman ASL-P270-866 Mary Nan Gamble Collection, Alaska State Library] *Arville Schaleben wrote more than 150 articles and took over 400 photographs of the colonists, his are among the best records of the project.*

THE MATANUSKA COLONY ALBUM

Fred Fordham, W.P.A. Motion Picture Record Division, on duty in Alaska. Letttering on machinery: F. E. R. A. Palmer, Alaska. [Willis T. Geisman ASL-P270-867 Mary Nan Gamble Collection, Alaska State Library]

THE MATANUSKA COLONY ALBUM

Madeleine de Foras, Red Cross nurse on one of her health visits, stops at the new cabin of John Meehan, colonist from Minnesota. Colonist Meehan hasconstructed a very attractive porch and entrance to his cabin. [Willis T. Geisman ASL-P270-614 Mary Nan Gamble Collection, Alaska State Library]

THE MATANUSKA COLONY ALBUM

L. L. Bell, colonist of Minnesota, sawing his winter's supply of wood. [Willis T. Geisman ASL-P270-617 Mary Nan Gamble Collection, Alaska State Library]

THE MATANUSKA COLONY ALBUM

Robert Biller and son, Bobby Jr., of Wisconsin carrying water to his tent. [Willis T. Geisman ASL-P270-618 Mary Nan Gamble Collection, Alaska State Library]

THE MATANUSKA COLONY ALBUM

With most of the colonists' tents on the site of their homesteads, the families can watch and assist in the building of their homes and also work on their land. [Willis T. Geisman ASL-P270-621 Mary Nan Gamble Collection, Alaska State Library]

THE MATANUSKA COLONY ALBUM

Colonist hauling logs for his cabin. [Willis T. Geisman ASL-P270-637 Mary Nan Gamble Collection, Alaska State Library]

THE MATANUSKA COLONY ALBUM

Two colonist children at play. [Willis T. Geisman ASL-P270-641 Mary Nan Gamble Collection, Alaska State Library]

THE MATANUSKA COLONY ALBUM

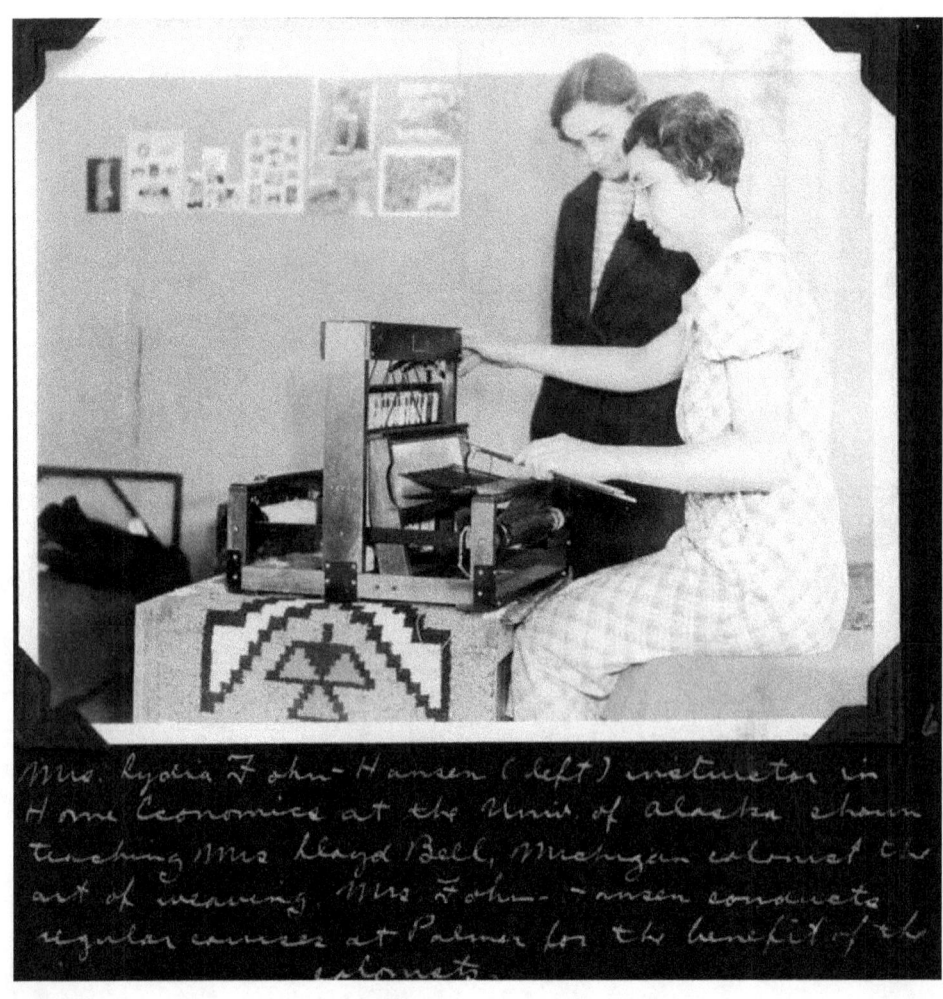

Mrs. Lydia Fohn-Hansen (left), instructor in Home Economics at the University of Alaska, shown teaching Mrs. Lloyd Bell, Michigan colonist, the art of weaving. Mrs. Fohn-Hansen conducts regular courses at Palmer for the benefit of the colonists. [Willis T. Geisman ASL-P270-642 Mary Nan Gamble Collection, Alaska State Library]

THE MATANUSKA COLONY ALBUM

Mrs. S. Jodin [Sjodin] of Minnesota smiles gayly as she runs the wash through her gasoline-driven Maytag washing machine. [Willis T. Geisman ASL-P270-644 Mary Nan Gamble Collection, Alaska State Library]

Colonist women hanging out their wash. [Willis T. Geisman ASL-P270-645a Mary Nan Gamble Collection, Alaska State Library]

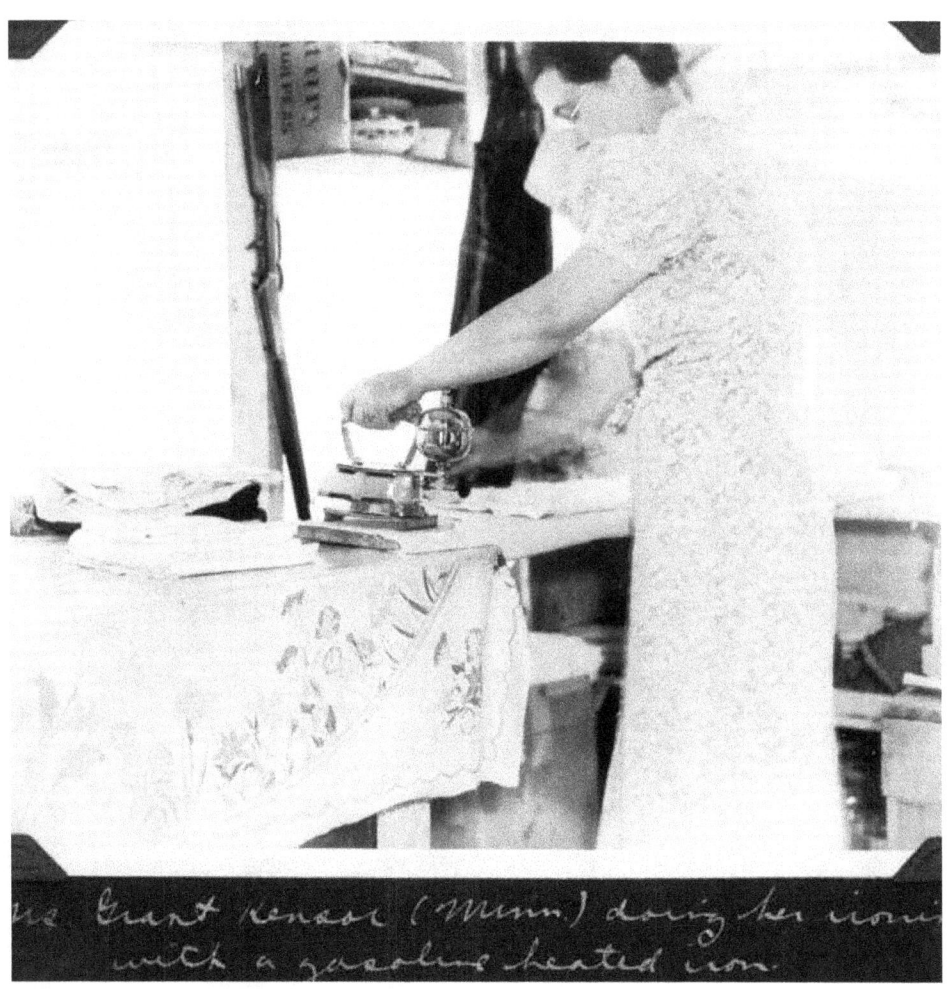

Mrs. Grant Kensor [Kenser] (Minn.) doing her ironing with a gasoline heated iron. [Willis T. Geisman ASL-P270-645b Mary Nan Gamble Collection, Alaska State Library]

Mrs. Carl Erickson (Minn.) shown in her neat kitchen in her tent home at Camp 8. [Willis T. Geisman ASL-P270-646 Mary Nan Gamble Collection, Alaska State Library]

Ruth Cook, colonist, taking in her wash. [Willis T. Geisman ASL-P270-649 Mary Nan Gamble Collection, Alaska State Library]

THE MATANUSKA COLONY ALBUM

Town scene near the warehouse at Palmer. France boy in wagon with hat. [Willis T. Geisman ASL-P270-647 Mary Nan Gamble Collection, Alaska State Library]

THE MATANUSKA COLONY ALBUM

Unloading freight at Palmer. [Willis T. Geisman ASL-P270-653 Mary Nan Gamble Collection, Alaska State Library]

THE MATANUSKA COLONY ALBUM

Mr. E. Huseby, colonist, peeling the bark off the logs on his cabin with a homemade tool that he constructed from a hoe. [Willis T. Geisman ASL-P270-654 Mary Nan Gamble Collection, Alaska State Library]

Yard scene at one of the new cabins.[Willis T. Geisman ASL-P270-655 Mary Nan Gamble Collection, Alaska State Library]

Well drill at work. [Willis T. Geisman ASL-P270-928 Mary Nan Gamble Collection, Alaska State Library]

THE MATANUSKA COLONY ALBUM

Full view of well drill. [Willis T. Geisman ASL-P270-929 Mary Nan Gamble Collection, Alaska State Library]

THE MATANUSKA COLONY ALBUM

Jimmie Ellsworth, young colonist from Michigan, and his steed.[Willis T. Geisman ASL-P270-668 Mary Nan Gamble Collection, Alaska State Library]

THE MATANUSKA COLONY ALBUM

Colonist women working in Community Garden at Camp 2. [Willis T. Geisman ASL-P270-679 Mary Nan Gamble Collection, Alaska State Library]
Camp no. 2 was located several miles southwest of Palmer, just west of the Matanuska Experiment Station on Trunk Road.

Cultivating at Community Garden. [Willis T. Geisman ASL-P270-682 Mary Nan Gamble Collection, Alaska State Library]

Colonist children picking raspberries. These berries abound in the area, and it is possible to pick a pail full in a very short time. [Willis T. Geisman ASL-P270-715 Mary Nan Gamble Collection, Alaska State Library]

THE MATANUSKA COLONY ALBUM

Mrs. Anna [Emma] Havemeister, colonist mother, and her family working in a garden near her home. Collection notes: Name is Emma – not Anna. [Willis T. Geisman ASL-P270-718 Mary Nan Gamble Collection, Alaska State Library]

THE MATANUSKA COLONY ALBUM

Barnyard scene. In the background is a colonist's tent home. [Willis T. Geisman ASL-P270-735 Mary Nan Gamble Collection, Alaska State Library]

Mrs. Rudolph Leander (left) of Minn. and Mrs. Johan Johnson of Minn. exhibit the lettuce and beets that they gathered in the garden. [Willis T. Geisman ASL-P270-742 Mary Nan Gamble Collection, Alaska State Library]

Mrs. E. W. Barry, colonist mother of seven children, proudly displays part of her 140 cans of salmon that she has recently put up. [Willis T. Geisman ASL-P270-748 Mary Nan Gamble Collection, Alaska State Library]

THE MATANUSKA COLONY ALBUM

W. Ising, Minnesota colonist, inspects the salmon in his smokehouse. Caught in the Matanuska River about a mile from his house, the dried salmon will make excellent food for the winter. [Willis T. Geisman ASL-P270-749 Mary Nan Gamble Collection, Alaska State Library]

A typical farm scene in the Matanuska Farm colony. Mrs. E. Huseby, colonist mother, in the garden behind her tent home picking turnips. In the backgroundcan be seen the Huseby's cabin in construction and their cattle. [Willis T. Geisman ASL-P270-754 Mary Nan Gamble Collection, Alaska State Library]

THE MATANUSKA COLONY ALBUM

E. Huseby with his son and dog in the small garden in the rear of his tent. [Willis T. Geisman ASL-P270-759 Mary Nan Gamble Collection, Alaska State Library]

THE MATANUSKA COLONY ALBUM

E. Huseby with his son and dog in the small garden in the rear of his tent. [Willis T. Geisman ASL-P270-759 Mary Nan Gamble Collection, Alaska State Library]

Mess Hall. [Willis T. Geisman ASL-P270-880 Mary Nan Gamble Collection, Alaska State Library]

THE MATANUSKA COLONY ALBUM

Francis Valley, cook in the Construction Corps, at one of the two stoves in the main camp on which the food for about 450 men is cooked. [Willis T. Geisman ASL-P270-900 Mary Nan Gamble Collection, Alaska State Library]

THE MATANUSKA COLONY ALBUM

Bake shop, Main Camp, Construction Corps. [Willis T. Geisman ASL-P270-901 Mary Nan Gamble Collection, Alaska State Library]

Bread oven in bake shop, main camp Construction Corps. [Willis T. Geisman ASL-P270-902 Mary Nan Gamble Collection, Alaska State Library]

Wm. Taylor (left) and two assistants standing beside a double boiler that they contrived to supply hot water for the 500 men in camp. [Willis T. Geisman ASL-P270-898 Mary Nan Gamble Collection, Alaska State Library]

Wash room. Construction Corps. Constructed by plumbing crew. [Willis T. Geisman ASL-P270-899 Mary Nan Gamble Collection, Alaska State Library]

Claude Hess, Minn. colonist, sharpening his axe before going to work on his land. [Willis T. Geisman ASL-P270-762 Mary Nan Gamble Collection, Alaska State Library]

Hay mower in Corporation hay field. [Willis T. Geisman ASL-P270-767 Mary Nan Gamble Collection, Alaska State Library]

THE MATANUSKA COLONY ALBUM

Harvesting oats. [Willis T. Geisman ASL-P270-769 Mary Nan Gamble Collection, Alaska State Library]

THE MATANUSKA COLONY ALBUM

Government horses being taken to pasture. [Willis T. Geisman ASL-P270-795 Mary Nan Gamble Collection, Alaska State Library]

Colonist taking horses to pasture. [Willis T. Geisman ASL-P270-806 Mary Nan Gamble Collection, Alaska State Library]

THE MATANUSKA COLONY ALBUM

An old settler's cow in pasture. [Willis T. Geisman ASL-P270-809 Mary Nan Gamble Collection, Alaska State Library]

Resembling a western prairie, this photograph shows another contrast that can be found in Alaska. Cows grazing on Cottonwood Flats. [Willis T. Geisman ASL-P270-812 Mary Nan Gamble Collection, Alaska State Library]

THE MATANUSKA COLONY ALBUM

Horses grazing on excellent pasture on the Flats. [Willis T. Geisman ASL-P270-813 Mary Nan Gamble Collection, Alaska State Library]

THE MATANUSKA COLONY ALBUM

Additional stacks of wild hay put up by the Corporation on Cottonwood Flats. [Willis T. Geisman ASL-P270-814 Mary Nan Gamble Collection, Alaska State Library]

Cottonwood Flats rented by the Corporation as a source of winter pasture. Knik Arm in the background. [Willis T. Geisman ASL-P270-816 Mary Nan Gamble Collection, Alaska State Library]

Robert Lathrop, an old settler, cutting hay on Cottonwood Flats with a pair of Corporation mares. [Willis T. Geisman ASL-P270-818 Mary Nan Gamble Collection, Alaska State Library]

Colonist shoeing a team. [Willis T. Geisman ASL-P270-826 Mary Nan Gamble Collection, Alaska State Library]

THE MATANUSKA COLONY ALBUM

Don L. Irwin, General Manager A.R.R.C. [Willis T. Geisman ASL-P270-828 Mary Nan Gamble Collection, Alaska State Library]
Don Irwin wrote a book about the colony, 'The Colorful Matanuska Valley'

THE MATANUSKA COLONY ALBUM

(L to R) Col. L. P. Hunt, Governor John W. Troy of Alaska, and Don L. Irwin, Gen. Mgr., A.R.R.C. [Willis T. Geisman ASL-P270-845 Mary Nan Gamble Collection, Alaska State Library]

Division heads, A.R.R.C. (L to R) A. M. Goodman, Eugene Carr, Dr. E. A. Ostrom, Don L. Irwin, Col. L P. Hunt, Alan Perkins, Ross Sheely. [Willis T. Geisman ASL-P270-851 Mary Nan Gamble Collection, Alaska State Library]

THE MATANUSKA COLONY ALBUM

Technical experts (L to R). Captain Parsons, U.S.N.; F. L. Biggs; Dr. R. G. Davis; Anton Anderson; Col. Hunt; S. R. Fuller; Dave Williams. [Willis T. Geisman ASL-P270-834 Mary Nan Gamble Collection, Alaska State Library]

THE MATANUSKA COLONY ALBUM

Construction Division Staff. [Willis T. Geisman ASL-P270-831 Mary Nan Gamble Collection, Alaska State Library]

Note photographer Willis T. Geisman on the left rear, standing

THE MATANUSKA COLONY ALBUM

The Construction Corps turns into a Skeleton City, Oct. 22nd [1935]. [Willis T. Geisman ASL-P270-906 Mary Nan Gamble Collection, Alaska State Library]

THE MATANUSKA COLONY ALBUM

Bibliography

Alanen, Arnold R. *Midwesterners in the Matanuska Valley: Colonizing Rural Alaska During the 1930s* (Article. People, Power, Places. University of Tennessee Press, Knoxville, TN 2000)

Fox, James. *The First Summer: Photographs of the Matanuska Colony of 1935* (Alaska Rural Rehabilitation Corporation, Palmer, AK 1980)

Geisman, Willis T. Mary Nan Gamble photograph collection. 976 b&w photographs documenting the Matanuska Colony Project. (Alaska State Archives, Alaska State Historical Library)

Hegener, Helen. *The Matanuska Colony Barns* (Northern Light Media, AK 2013)
 –*The 1935 Matanuska Colony Project* (Northern Light Media, AK 2014)

Irwin, Don. *The Colorful Matanuska Valley* (Don Irwin, AK 1968)

Johnson, Hugh A., and Stanton, Keith L. *Matanuska Valley Memoir: The Story of How One Alaskan Community Developed* (University of Alaska Experiment Station, Palmer, AK 1955)

Miller, Orlando W. *The Frontier in Alaska and the Matanuska Colony* (Yale University Press, New Haven, CT 1975)

THE MATANUSKA COLONY ALBUM

The Matanuska Colony Album
by Helen Hegener

Additional copies of this book
are available for $24.00 postpaid from:

> Northern Light Media
> PO Box 298023
> Wasilla, Alaska 99629
>
> http://northernlightmedia.wordpress.com
> email: northernlightmedia@gmail.com

Other titles available from Northern Light Media

- *The Matanuska Colony Barns*
- *The 1935 Matanuska Colony Project*
- *The Beautiful Matanuska Valley*
- *Along Alaskan Trails: Adventures in Sled Dog History*
- *The All Alaska Sweepstakes: History of the Great Race*
- *Long Hard Trails and Sled Dog Tales*
- *Appetite & Attitude: A Conversation with Lance Mackey* (DVD)

www.ingramcontent.com/pod-product-compliance
Lightning Source LLC
Chambersburg PA
CBHW071440160426
43195CB00013B/1977